REAL WORLD

505

LEADER GUIDE

REAL WORLD
505

LEADER GUIDE

ALCOTT
GERMANY II

CITI OF BOOKS

CITIOFBOOKS, INC.
3736 Eubank NE Suite A1
Albuquerque, NM 87111-3579
www.citiofbooks.com

Hotline: 1 (877) 389-2759
Fax: 1 (505) 930-7244

Ordering Information:
Quantity sales. Special discounts are available on quantity purchases by corporations, associations, and others. For details, contact the publisher at the address above.

Printed in the United States of America.

ISBN-13:	Paperback	979-8-89391-656-0
	Hardback	979-8-89391-657-7
	eBook	979-8-89391-658-4

Library of Congress Control Number: 2025908137

Table of Contents

Preface 1

Introduction 5

Action #1 - Understand. 12

    The Jerk Boss.... 12

    Stand in front, not in the way. 20

    So... why lead and why you? 23

Action # 2 Engage 24

    Where it starts and stops 24

    The Race Track Analogy 27

    So, who's to blame? 29

Action # 3 Trust 31

    Outside-in versus Inside-Out 31

    Trust Over Control 37

    Intentional Diversity 42

Action #4 Translate. 47

    Translate versus Communicate 47

    The Art of Translation 52

    The Willingness and Ability to Teach.. 54

As we end. 57

    Laying it all on the line 57

    Until next time 59

References 61

About the Author. 62

Preface

I cannot believe fifteen years have passed since we last talked during the days of *Real World 101: Student Guide*! I must admit, that was an awesome time with some great discussion. Real World 101 gave us a chance to highlight the importance of questioning everything and use that knowledge to drive us towards our purpose. Questioning everything is powerful and making informed decisions for yourself prepares the world for you instead of the other way around. For those readers picking up this book without reading Real World 101, that was the gist of the conversation without giving away a ton of detail. I encourage you to join in that discussion and give your own thoughts on it when you have the time. Until then, welcome aboard.

So, why keep the conversation going? Why come back after 15 years? All fair questions. To be honest, I had not realized fifteen years had passed until I started writing at this moment. The cliché of time flying is a total understatement. Although you probably did not get this book for free, money was not my motivation either. I am just too passionate about this subject to make it about money. The motivating factor for this conversation is you. The encouraging words I received from Real World 101 readers asking for more content. The aspiring leaders, educators, and others trying to grow their careers without sacrificing their integrity, trusted me as their mentor and inspired me to have this discussion with you. Seeing others reach their dreams just by learning from experiences and lessons I can share is one life's greatest rewards for me. It is what inspired me to write Real World 101 and why Real World 505 stayed on my mind, even after 15 years. There was no grand plan to wait this long. Initially, I thought I would author this book within five years of publishing Real World 101. By then, at the ripe age of thirty-three, I believed I had figured everything out. This probably sounds like something we all say when coming out of our twenties and rolling into thirty. It is amazing what we all think we know, even when we ask all the right questions (what's this for? what now? what next?) to all the right people. By age thirty, I had degrees from strong programs and career success in multiple industries at some of the largest companies in the world. After being battle tested in my career and in life with issues involving classism, racism, and personal uncertainty, I learned that overcoming each of these obstacles only matters if others can learn and surpass what you were able to do in your own time. This is why keeping the conversation going matters most.

For fifteen years, my life's journey drove me to focus on my choices, my family, and my purpose, always knowing that one day we would reconnect and share our ideas and experiences again. Over that time, I experienced triumphant moments and tragedy. Before I knew it, I was the Vice President in one of the largest organizations in the country, leading the way for others to be their best selves. I had a chance to apply everything we talked about in Real World 101 coupled with some new lessons along the way - and it worked! I even have a family of my own now (wife, son, two daughters), which enables me to appreciate the power of purpose in more ways than I ever imagined. That said, if I have learned anything in this time, it is that the journey is far from over and before I continue down my path, I want to lift my head up to see how things are going with you. By the time we finish this discussion, I hope to answer some of your questions and inspire you to do the same for someone else.

So, what are we going to talk about? Something worthwhile? Yes indeed. This is a topic that everyone on the planet deals with in one form or another. It is something that exists in our human fabric, for ourselves and even for others. It requires you to make important choices, whether you want the responsibility or not. The topic we are going to discuss is **leadership**. Whether for yourself or for others, leadership is an unavoidable responsibility we all must deal with, no matter the personality type. You may wonder if being in the spotlight makes you a leader, it does not. The role of a leader is to bring together perspective and action for the purpose of driving change. How you lead is driven by who you want to be as a person and how you respond to the challenges that occur in your life's journey. Moments in your leadership journey can be fun, exciting, and scary all at once. As we talk through these moments, you will see for yourself. Our conversation will challenge you on what it means to be the leader you want to be, instead of becoming the leader others say you should.

Thank you for committing to this discussion. Real World 505 is officially in session....

Introduction

Tying Connections to Outcomes

Set the stage – Be honest with yourself.

The path to impactful leadership extends beyond the basics of addressing an audience and delivering inspiring words or being the person courageous enough to make the final decision. Often, we hear about the importance of "people" and that they are the most important asset in an organization. If that is true, then the essence of great leadership should center on how well a leader impacts people. Seems obvious, right? The idea is clear, but consistently showing up for "the people" is not so easy.

In this discussion, we will uncover the intangibles that make up strong leaders. We will explore the commitment needed to build impactful leadership, which can seem complicated and may require more of your persona than you anticipated. Our discussion will reveal the most vital leadership components to drive the two biggest qualities anyone can appreciate in a strong leader: *connections* and *outcomes*. Creating connections while delivering outcomes of any kind makes leadership impactful and truly worthwhile.

Think about this before we get started:

How can I connect people from various backgrounds, both similar and different from my own, to a single outcome?

Consider what it is like to connect a single person, who thinks differently than you, to an outcome you envision. Then with ten people. Now, imagine if that ten becomes a hundred, then a thousand. Contrary to widespread belief, leaders everywhere are expected to think this way, but we both know this is not how all leaders approach their responsibility. Yet, from this perspective, we can begin to appreciate the art of leadership and how it involves bringing people together while also making the complicated look simple. I know, fun times, right? What is the magic trick that allows us to pull that off repeatedly? Before delving into the dense layers that come with answering this question, we will start by addressing a more important question: **Why lead and why you?** Being honest with yourself about this will allow you to decide where we will go with this discussion and the steps you will take when going through your leadership journey. Think about it. If you cannot be honest with yourself, how can you require honesty from others as a leader? Purposeful reflection on why you want to lead and why that leader should be you sets the stage for embracing the rest of this discussion.

Understand, Engage, Trust, and Translate....

We will spend our time covering these leadership actions:

1. Understand

2. Engage

3. Trust

4. Translate

I tried to make a catchy acronym for these topics without coming off quirky or falling into a cliché - totally bombed. I am seriously still open to suggestions. Regardless, I am confident that these actions will stick with you after we discuss how to apply these intangibles to your leadership journey.

As we break down how to apply each topic, you will see the depth that comes with unpacking these methods and applying them in ways that matter most to you and the people you lead. We will discuss how to apply **understanding** and how to use it for more than just observing from afar and asking surface-level questions. We will talk about how understanding starts first with you, then the team (trust me, I am not giving too much away, there is more). This part of the discussion will give you the foundation needed for the topics to follow: *engagement, trust,* and *translation.*

When we discuss **engagement**, we will talk about how to drive stability in a team by embracing new interactions. First-time or unfamiliar engagements can be nerve-racking because of the fear of the unknown. You will get a chance to think through how not to allow this type of fear to be a factor because embracing the unknown is what you want for yourself and your team. By the time we finish this chapter, you will see what it means to stand in front without standing in the way.

Next, we will talk about the connection between **trust** and leadership. Anyone can speak on the importance of trust when it comes to leadership. I mean, who openly talks about effective leadership without saying the word "trust" a few times? Everyone knows how bad it sounds to leave trust out of leadership, but still, we see a lack of trust in many places, especially where we work. When we unpack this topic, you will see what happens when trust comes face to face with our human desire to control. You will find many leaders who do not see trust and control as conflicting principles seem to have some of the biggest issues with team morale. Are you able to imagine empowerment or diverse thinking consistently embraced in an environment void of trust? You may be surprised how often all leaders struggle with this (yes, including you). We will see how something that sounds so simple to preserve can still be tough to do and what steps you can take to ensure your actions don't compromise something this important.

Communication, communication, communication, a word we all hear more times than we can count, especially in leadership circles.

I am sure you wake up with the desire to hear these every day:

- *"Let's work on our communication. "*

- *"We just need to be better communicators."*

- *"You need to be clearer in your communication."*

How often have you heard those repetitive lines?

More so, how often do we respond with saying (or thinking) the lines below with the same unwanted results?

- *"I sent the email."*

- *"Did you get my text?"*

- *"Why don't you pick up the phone?"*

- *"I told them this already, why don't they get it?"*

Let's talk about it (I know – too soon?). After discussing how to understand, engage, and trust, we will talk about the difference between **translating** a message instead of just communicating it.

Understanding, engagement, trust, and translation are the building blocks that you will find useful when generating connections to create outcomes, not only in others but within yourself as well. We will see how these methods can make the complexities that come with leadership more simple, enjoyable, and fulfilling. Trust me, it will be fun...

Bias and Diversity

Throughout our discussion, we will hit on one element of leadership that so many perceive to be an add-on – **an intentional focus on diversity**. Our leadership journeys allow us to encounter people from various backgrounds and experiences in organizations both large and small. No matter how widespread our experiences are, bias is still an inherited part of who we are as human beings. This is why breaking that mindset must come with intentionality. In our discussion, we will see how a lack of intentional focus on diversity will limit your ability to innovate and minimize the impact of the four leadership actions (understand, engage, trust, translate). We will also see how an active leadership focus to build diverse teams and interactions is not an add-on concept, but a mandate for anyone looking to be a part of something bigger than themselves.

As I conclude this introduction, I ask you to make this commitment – create questions for yourself as we cover each topic. It is the best way for this book to provide you value. I will have my share of thought questions for you, but the most important aspect of this book is for you to author your own leadership journey. Let us use this time in the chapters ahead to challenge our thinking and change the world in ways only your dreams can uncover. I hope once again that this is another fun read where I can support your leadership journey by challenging your thoughts with a few of my own…

Understand

The Jerk Boss...

Let's dive right into the first action of leadership – **understanding**. Building your ability to understand as a leader involves many layers. What does it mean to even grow in understanding? Let's start by discussing one of the biggest obstacles that gets in the way of leading, even with the best intentions – our egos. Yes, our own worst enemy to greatness starts with ourselves.

How can that be the case? Consider this:

Countless professions including authors, speakers, and teachers share the notion that before you can lead others, you must first understand what it means to follow. I am guilty of saying this a time or two myself. Sometimes it just helps to tell yourself this to prevent your ego from getting the best of you. I am certain you can name at least one high-standing leader (even the one you see in the mirror) who constantly comes off as someone who places their views above everyone else's. Does seeing this kind of behavior make this leader a bad person? – it might. Does this mean that one day a person who leads this way will get what's coming to them? Some of us think this way often, but what in the world does that even mean? You have probably witnessed individuals with unchecked egos still have career success. Good. It is important to accept that having an ego that personally drives you to have ambition is not a bad thing. Leaders who rely solely on the efforts of others without placing any value on people can still attain career success. Let's also admit that many organizations believe the assertiveness of a person with large egotistical characteristics is a winning formula for leadership, no matter how vile the behavior. Why? Because that approach can still produce bottom-line financial gains to that organization. So, it is fair to say, nor is it a crime, for a business to try to stay in business. What gets overlooked is the collateral damage of this approach. A sustained dose of this type of leadership may benefit you individually, but it will also deteriorate the culture of the organization. Before you know it your team's morale, culture, and productivity dwindle to a halt, each unable to recover without a costly overhaul. So what reason is there to speak against leading with an overly wild ego? Investing in yourself isn't the worst thing to do. Aren't your aspirations as important as anyone else's? When you see someone able to attain wealth and notoriety by being a jerk, why not be callous and self-centered? Why not let your ego get the best of you and just climb that organizational ladder at the expense of others? I mean, look at the size of that house!

You're probably thinking at this moment,

*"What does this writer want me to take from this? First, he tells me that having an ego is natural, then he says I can ruin an organization with my ego, but then investing in myself is something I want to do. Is the writer trying to sell me on the idea that I can be a **jerk boss** and still have success or not?"*

Fair questions. What I want you to see is that there are multiple schools of thought on answering an important question you need to pose to yourself, but before we get to that, I want to assure you that all leaders and executives are not jerks and pursuing career success with driven ambition does not make you a jerk boss. I would also be the biggest hypocrite if I tried to convince you that career success can only come if you are a jerk. Attempting to make that point would give you every reason to immediately walk away now before we even get into some good conversation.

So why bring this up? To point out that a crucial step in your leadership journey starts with knowing and embracing your leadership identity. What would you say to yourself when asked, *what kind of leader do you want to be?* How would you even begin to describe it? Whether you decide to be a jerk boss or not, you must understand this question and answer it for yourself. The commitment you make to your response will hold you accountable to your own leadership style and prevent you from basing your leadership behaviors solely on what you see other leaders do.

The jerk boss prioritizes self, typically with little to no regard for how their decisions impact the stability, production, or morale of a team or organization. This person believes that whatever they think is what others should do and what is good for that leader is what is good for everyone. With the jerk boss, you will typically see a pattern where the next shiny thing that highlights their individual greatness becomes the priority, and the growth, development, and effectiveness of the team become an afterthought. Now let's be honest, we've all been there in one form or another where our egos have gotten the best of us. Remember how it felt when that job, relationship, car, or whatever that "thing" was you wanted, was so important to you that you did not want to even consider the risk. Collateral damage, logic, and reason didn't matter as much in those instances either. It was about you and whatever it took to get what you deserved. This kind of feeling is so rewarding and common to everyone, which is why it is important to understand this behavior without embracing it or judging others for it. The question to consider is, what happens when this behavior goes unchecked? when the focus of the team's success becomes all about you, but failure is directed towards all those "important" team members who just need to step up. An unchecked ego

If everyone just follows my lead, works hard, and does whatever it takes just like me, we'll win!" This doesn't sound so convincing when you say it out loud.

enables this illusion, or better yet, delusion. Before you know it, team morale is low, the working environment is toxic, and you never even noticed. Afterwards, team performance is poor with no understanding of why and instead of looking in the mirror, your search aimlessly, trying to find the source of the problem.

Before you attempt to convince yourself that you can't be the jerk boss, challenge yourself to see if these are questions you ask yourself at that start of the day:

1. What am I trying to accomplish with my team?

2. What am I doing to set my team up for success?

3. What is the outcome for everyone when we win?

Take your responses and apply them to the diagram on the next page. I'm calling the diagram the *Jerk Boss Spectrum*. After answering the questions and using the diagram, where did you fall on it? Does your leadership tend to lend itself towards the jerk boss or not?

JERK BOSS SPECTRUM

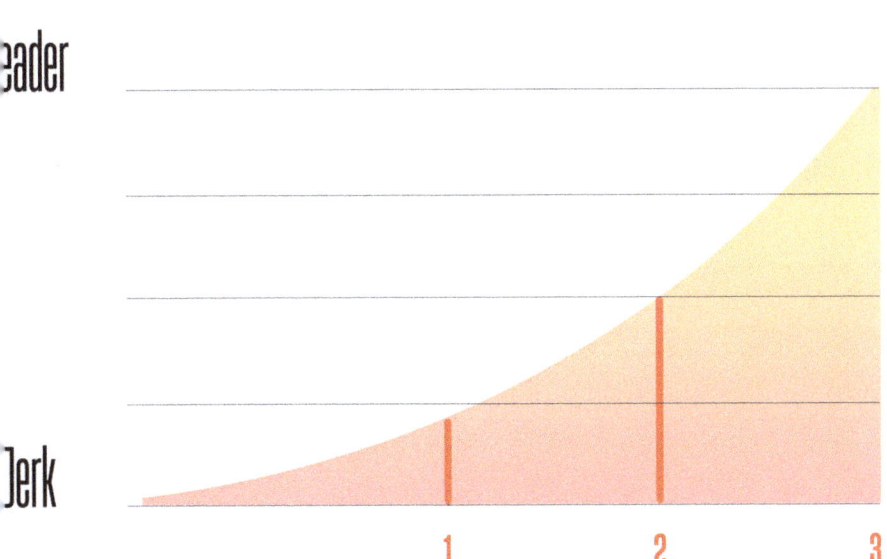

1. What am I trying to accomplish?

Do you understand what your team needs to accomplish and why it matters?

2. What am I doing to set the team up for success?

What actions will you take to ensure the team is successful?

3. What is the outcome for everyone?

Do you know how the outcomes of the work will benefit everyone involved?

Don't be hard on yourself. Everyone has at least some Jerk Boss in them. This simple exercise is not intended to condescend or judge, but to prepare yourself for this question:

Why should I be the one to lead this team through these challenges?

We talked earlier about leadership identity. This is the part of the conversation where your purpose and your leadership identity should begin to converge. The question above forces you to better understand your leadership intentions and provide insight into what it will take for you to lead with integrity.

Egos are not inherently bad. We all have them. Unchecked egos prevent you from connecting with your team and helping others thrive. Are you committed to being the jerk boss, or a leader that grows people and organizations using healthy connections? Be honest with yourself when you answer. Your response will shape your thinking in the chapters ahead.

Embrace Complexity - Preserve the Secret Sauce

Breaking news! People are complicated. Although it is an obvious thing to say, it is still tough to accept. No two human beings (except for identical twins perhaps), think exactly alike about everything. Our natural behavior is to build teams with people who think in ways you do. That makes sense. When you can find people with similar behaviors, learning styles and beliefs, interactions are not as complex. Finding a person with similar interests and habits to you is also not a crime. However, this approach comes at a price. When building relationships, it is the differences between us and others that matter the most. Complexity is a good thing and something you want to have on your team. Why? Because it is the complexity in people that drives innovation, effective collaboration, and new discoveries. Just go back forty years, the idea of a drone delivering groceries or even online learning being a standard practice for education at all levels was nothing short of imaginary. These developments started with diverse thought and imagination, then with technical skill and execution. People thinking the same way may have led to larger school buildings instead of online learning or faster delivery trucks instead of drone transports. Avoiding complex interactions may feel comforting, but it also limits our ability to bring innovative ideas to the forefront with challenging debates and new perspectives. The complexity in people enables healthy tension that comes with our differences and where the *secret sauce* resides to embark on historical breakthroughs.

Understanding is vital to showing others that our greatest value is not in our similarities, but in our differences.

Not wasting the secret sauce requires you to embrace healthy tension and understand behaviors that dilute creative differences. Avoid actions that force members of your team to think exactly how you would. Do not smother the creative differences that allow your team to be historically great.

Ensure you are creating guideposts for creativity and not boundaries. Building your awareness around these practices will drive how you act on them, which we will discuss further in the chapters ahead.

Stand in front, not in the way

Have you ever been asked by someone to stand in front of a line, but be sure not to get in the way? Try saying this to someone waiting in line at the airport and see where that gets you. *Standing in front but not in the way* may sound a bit eccentric, but this approach is so effective when exercising your ability to understand your team and organization as a leader.

So how do you know when you are not in the way, but leading from the front? Here are some observations you will need to consider to help guide you to that answer.

1. Do you see everyone on your team open and respectful, especially when challenging one another?

2. Do you see everyone talking about problems without pointing fingers or the fear of repercussion?

3. Do you see everyone supporting each other without being told to do so?

4. Do you see everyone celebrating each other's accomplishments as individuals and as a team?

5. Do you see everyone excited for the next challenge?

If you can answer yes to questions 1-5, you can safely assume that you are not wasting secret sauce and you are not standing in the way of your team's growth. If you cannot answer yes to all five questions, that doesn't mean you have a bad team or that you are an inadequate leader. What it indicates is where to begin your efforts to understand your team, get closer to the team, or areas you may want to adjust your leadership style. Remember, the complexity that comes with people will not allow for each one of these questions to become a "yes" overnight. Practice your willingness to challenge and share ideas, especially towards yourself from others. This kind of behavior will resonate in your team's desire to proactively contribute and display their talents without the fears that come with micromanagement and leadership approval. The collaborative behaviors you witness will validate your ability to understand your team and the enjoyable results that come along with it.

Strategies, missions, and visions – Yes, they are important. Just don't stop there!

There are countless resources and guides that illustrate how to develop and verbalize a strategy. However, no matter how visually appealing the presentation, execution will consistently fall short if there is no effort to connect your strategy with the capabilities of your team. The team's ability to execute will always suffer when a strategy does not connect with a team's capability. No matter how loud or catchy your rally-cry slogans are, the team will tune you out when the team consistently cannot deliver. Consider a sports team with a losing record. Over time, fan attendance drops, and you start to see a lack of effort from the team itself. Later you notice that the sports team does just enough for the check to clear. Why? Because everyone begins to see that the team was not built to win, despite the slogans and goals posted on the wall at the start of the year. Without taking the action to understand how your team can accomplish the goal, losses will pile up, morale will suffer, and your team's productivity will decline. As a leader, the action to understand is about challenging yourself to consistently connect your goals with the people who will execute them. Understand the makeup of your team and how to make them successful in their role.

Helpful thoughts to consider when connecting strategy with capability:

1. What's the ultimate goal? What does it look like to win the championship?

2. Why is achieving this goal so important for you? What should it mean for the team?

3. What is your team's superpower i.e., what makes your team great?

4. How do you know if you are set up to deliver on this strategy?

5. How do you ensure the team is set up for success?

The actions you take to Understand yourself, your outcomes, and your team sets the stage for leading a high-performing environment capable of solving any problem. When you align these three areas, you can rally your team around any problem. This is what it truly means to stand in front, not in the way.

So... why lead and why you?

We covered several topics in this chapter to highlight the power and commitment that comes with the actions you take to understand yourself and your ecosystem as a leader. I hope you had a chance to see not just what understanding both provides, but why it is important. As we wrap up this chapter you should revisit the question – *Why lead and Why You?* Leading with integrity is not easy, but it is worthwhile. Ask yourself, are you willing to steer the boat while allowing the team to run the ship? Are you willing to take the responsibility to create an environment and drive outcomes instead of dictating everyone's personality? Does this kind of responsibility sound remotely enjoyable to you? If your answers are yes, then you've officially set the stage to become an impactful leader and not a jerk boss. Now that we've laid the groundwork on what kind of leader you want to be, let's discuss how to embrace our next leadership action – **engagement**.

Engage

Where it starts and stops

We had to first address the importance of understanding because it is vital to grasp problems, people, and most importantly, ourselves when leading. The real fun begins after that work is done. How often do you hear phrases like, "talk is cheap" or "I hear you talking but you're not saying anything?" Bottom line, great intentions are awesome to have when collaborating with people, but leadership, as in many things, requires engaging actions. Engaging actions are the best and probably the only message that matters when working with people to get things done.

Some of our greatest concerns stem from a fear of failure. Think back to that petrifying feeling you get when trying to overcome the anxiety you get at times when trying to prove yourself. Do not shy away from the reality that these feelings occur often and are a part of you. Anything worth pursuing should drive some sort of nervous energy. A job interview, a big-time promotion, or even a game can create anxious moments that feel like invisible weights keeping you from being confident, positive, or even taking a physical step forward. When leading others, these same feelings can exist, and yes, at times they should. Why? Because the decisions you make will have a direct impact on meaningful moments, starting with the team's morale, their journeys in life, and their ability to succeed.

In my travels, I've been a part of some hair-raising moments. I can recall a time when my team needed to fix a problem due to a total collapse in service delivery. Clients were upset, millions of dollars were lost, and our reputation was taking a hit. When that happens, morale can drop along with the confidence to persevere with positivity. We knew that this was a defining moment for us. Our next steps had to be our best or the company itself would be done for good. These are the moments when the engagement action thrives. **Engagement** is all about getting involved and standing in front of the problem, but not in the... oh well, you get it by now. – We've shared that thought already, so here is what it means to do it:

When engaging a team in either a calm or critical situation:

1. Avoid finger pointing. Solve the problem first!

2. Listen to the people doing the work.

3. Understand where the breakdowns are and why they happen.

4. Break away from old methods; replace them with new and better ways with your team.

5. Evaluate your solution and be sure it works.

We all would love to believe that as leaders, we can just lean on talent, clear direction, and a healthy delivery system to keep things on the up and up. If only leadership were that simple. When things are going well, this is a convenient description to give. However, the reality is that in any organization or team where you are pushing towards excellence, systems can go awry, results veer off, clients get upset, and tension mounts. This is where your power of engagement must emerge. Engagement requires you to be the initiator of change. The tone you set when approaching a problem can either instill or destroy a team's confidence. The belief you show in your team and in yourself is what will drive a healthy culture of accountability and innovation. In other words, the impact of your engagement and the role it plays starts and stops with you.

Own the Racetrack, not the driver – The Racetrack Analogy

The purpose of a racetrack is to provide every driver with guiderails to move forward in the same direction without forcing everyone to drive in the exact same way. When drivers fall off the pace, the pit crew acts. The actions of the pit crew can be as simple as refueling and changing a few tires or as intense as making massive adjustments to the framework of the racecar due to a collision. No matter what, the driver stops in the pit area, and the crew assesses and takes action to get the driver back on track. When there is total chaos on the track, caution flags rise for everyone to slow down. This allows all debris to clear, a new pace to be established, and for drivers to get back on track and move in the same direction again. For massive resets to happen like this, someone that every driver can trust with a reset must maintain awareness of the track and know when to intervene. Do you see why I like this analogy so much?

Think of yourself as the person leading the pit crew, holding the caution flag, or even driving the pace car. As a leader, you are not the racecar driver. You are responsible for the track. At times, you may want to course-correct a driver by "taking control of the wheel." However, kicking the driver out of their seat and driving their car will not help you ensure the other drivers are getting what they need to be a part of the race. A *"kick the driver out the car"*

Sometimes our experience as leaders compels us to show others how we drive. Use that energy and passion to build new and better drivers.

mentality forces you to stand in the way, instead of leading from the front. Ensuring your drivers are set up for success is the engagement action that increases the capability of the driver and along with the harmony and speed of the track. Leadership engagement requires your overarching awareness, especially towards other race teams run by different leaders. Because in the end, we all want to have a great race so that the fans can come back to the track. Leadership engagement requires you to take on the challenge of helping every driver in the race without needing to jump in the car. Own the track, not the driver.

So how do we engage the driver and the track? Let's add some context to the five engagement actions we discussed earlier using our racetrack analogy.

Start by listening to the people doing the work. Listening to the drivers will give you the best insight into how the track runs and where changes are necessary. Once again, your goal is to keep everyone set up for success. Learn about your drivers and where their greatest difficulties are on the track. The entire raceway is your ecosystem, and the breakdowns can be anywhere. Be open to learning where they are, especially in areas you never considered.

Stay open to new thoughts and ideas. The perspective of the track owner is different from that of the crew chiefs and drivers. This means perspectives, complexities, and what others see daily are also different from yours. Take what you know and merge that knowledge with lessons learned from others. Do not feel the need to override opposing views just because they are different. Be open to the fact that what you fully understand may still only be a part of the story. The race looks a bit different from one driver's seat to the next. Getting things on track is your responsibility as the leader, but without talented drivers who trust you and whom you can trust, there is no race.

Lead the charge to break stereotypes and traditional thinking. Opposition comes with engagement, especially when breaking the *"we've always done things this way"* rule. Contrary to widespread belief, not everyone is a fan of change no matter how much we say we are. Just because engagement is the right thing to do does not mean it will always be the most fun. Use your engagement actions to change the status quo and build stronger connections between the driver and crew. Positive engagement keeps everyone working together and learning from one another as a team. As a leader you have the platform, so use it. Without it, you and your team will remain stuck running the same race with the same collisions every time.

So, who's to blame?

Have you thought of this at one time or another – "Why should I get blamed for someone else's mistakes?" Now that question is enough to spike up the anxiety levels. Nevertheless, let's look at this differently. Is it really someone else's mistake when it is your team? As the leader, you are accountable for the outcomes that your team produces, so would it not make sense to at least assume some of the blame when things go wrong? When things go great, who would you like others to see? Engagement and understanding go hand in hand when shaping yourself into the leader you want to be. Active leadership engagement requires you to create an environment that not only solves problems, but one that is built on trust, certainty, and common goals that impact everyone. Your acts of engagement are a means to hold yourself accountable for the environment you worked so hard to build. Would you really prefer someone else to fix something you believe reflects who you are? Use your engagement actions to be present with your team, business, or organization to emphasize your commitment to intentional and involved leadership. If this is not enjoyable on any level, then you may have just answered whether leading with integrity is something you desire. The people you lead and the goals you have are a package deal. For those who believe that strong leadership can come without active engagement, check out their teams. Then tell me how well they work and innovate together. I am willing to bet they are missing something. What is it? Well, that is a perfect segway to our next discussion topic – **trust**.

Trust

Outside In vs Inside Out

Trust is a leadership action that deserves its own spotlight. You might argue trust is the glue that keeps all the leadership actions together. Trust is a powerful word often considered essential in both leadership and life. It is what brings meaning to your understanding and transforms leadership engagement efforts into meaningful actions. Because it is such a powerful and influential word to use, I am certain you often see it applied in the most clichéd and ambiguous ways. We will discuss how to avoid this in the sections ahead and show how trust as a central focus of your leadership will determine if your possibilities are limited or limitless.

Some of the more basic forms of trust we take for granted all the time. When driving, we trust that drivers will follow most, if not all, driving laws. You trust that the roof of your home won't collapse on you at night. When boarding an aircraft, you trust the airline pilot to arrive safely and on time to your destination (okay, maybe just safely). Although these are basic examples, they illustrate the forms of trust we encounter most often. The pilot, your roof, other drivers—you name it. Much of the trust we appreciate often exists from the ***outside-in***, meaning you trust things will not happen to you because of what you expect to *receive from others*. There is a contrast that comes when embracing leadership. Trusted leaders stand out not because of what you see them receive, but because of the trust they *create for others*. The trust you create impacts the behaviors that others have toward each other. Your team will have reasons to trust one another when they see how much you trust them. This is what it means to build trust from the ***inside-out***. As we will discuss later in this chapter, the trust you create is most visible and needed in times of growth or conflict, rather than in times of prosperity.

Psychological Safety – Stay at the study table

When establishing trust. Start with placing an emphasis on psychological safety. Psychological safety unlocks possibilities for collaborative thought. When in school, some of my best learning experiences took place outside the classroom without an instructor. In these moments, the lessons that stuck with me the most took place at the study table with other students wrecking their brains just like me, obsessed with getting the right answer. With my classmates, it was easier to admit my faults and misconceptions. Hearing from other students willing to share their mental blocks, especially those struggling the same as I, created an environment of psychological safety that helped us all get the answers we needed in our own ways. We learned from one another, completed our assignments with high marks, and built relationships to last a lifetime. Why is that? Because in those moments, no one was afraid to fail. Safe spaces welcome the possibilities of diverse thought, opposing views, and mistakes. Creating psychological safety ensures healthy engagement that is not forced or disingenuous. Try buying a 1,000-piece puzzle set and try to assemble it in a public place or even at the store where you made the purchase. You are probably not feeling safe space vibes if you tried to put it together in the middle of the store with people looking over your shoulder. What if you took that same puzzle home with a couple of trusted friends? Think about how much easier and enjoyable it is to find those jigsaw pieces with everyone having a good time solving a complicated problem and learning from each other's mistakes. This is the environment you want to create with inside-out trust. The result of inside-out trust is psychological safety. Your team and organization will use psychological safety to connect with positivity and confidence. It also helps a team know for itself that they are solving problems amongst friends. How many times have you tried to force the wrong pieces together only to later move on to a different part of the puzzle? No one wants to feel judged by that (trust me, people would). The psychological safety you enable with inside-out trust keeps everyone focused on the problem, free from judgment. We've talked earlier about the importance of engagement and what it means to stand in front. Ensuring psychological safety is the cornerstone for establishing and maintaining the trust you need to lead and stay engaged from the front. There is a phrase that says *leaders bring the weather.* If that is true, how would others describe the temperature, visibility, and barometric pressure you bring?

Trusted or Liked

Not everyone who is trusted is liked, but not everyone who is liked is trusted. So, what is the difference, and which is better? Let's talk through it, then I'll leave that for you to decide.

Getting back to what we discussed earlier, your role as the leader is to create trust, not likeness. So, what's the difference? Building trust starts with the desire to connect with people. Objectivity, collaboration, transparency and common goals—these ingredients connect people using honest feedback and integrity. With this approach, your team will build connections with you and one another based on clear and aligned expectations. This environment creates the psychological safety we discussed earlier. Before long you will see an organic shift where your team will begin to like one another in the process. When focused on being liked, you skip these steps and spend your time catering solely to the emotions of people. There are some short-term relationship gains to this, but once a challenge comes and misaligns these emotions, you will have no foundation to fall back on (let the finger-pointing begin). Don't get me wrong, being liked can feel great, but without achievements and a sense of connection, those awesome feelings within the team will turn into toxic behavior quicker than you think. Why? – Because prioritizing likeness over trust forces you to steer your leadership approach from objectivity and direct engagement to a more subjective transparency when problems arise. Subjective transparency uses deflection instead of ownership, condescending comments over collaboration, and decisions driven by ego instead of by data and objectivity. The more subjective you become in your leadership, the greater the emphasis will be on loud opinions and, yes, bias.

Be conscious of your bias and a desire to be liked. When unchecked bias will ruin your ability to install trust and embrace opposing views.

When accountability measures kick up in an environment centered on likeness instead of trust, inconsistent expectations are set throughout the team. Now everyone on the team has a different reason for liking you and each other (remember that complexity thing we talked about?). You now have a toxic environment with no objective foundation, no trust. When the organizational needs shift, you must juggle all that subjectivity, then before you know it, firefighting, panic, wasted effort, and frustration becomes the norm. Congrats, you now win the grand prize of more finger pointing, more clichés (e.g., "Let's all get on the same page"— heard that one?), and jerk boss moves to manage the team. I wish I were making this up, but this happens often. If this has happened to you personally, feel free to laugh to keep from crying. Building trust takes work, but when you look at the alternative, it pays off in the long run.

Bottom line, toxic work environments based on likeness over trust when inside-out trust, psychological safety, and clear objectives are lacking. Without trust, there's nothing for the team or you to turn to when the tough moments come, and they will come. Establish trust in your teams to stabilize your team's ability to adapt when challenges arise. Once you have it, the team will look at you and one another without confusion or fear, regardless of the situation.

So…Would you still rather be liked? Give it some thought.

Creating trust requires you to be the ultimate equalizer capable of directing the tension everyone feels towards the problem instead of towards each other.

Here are some tactical ways to create trust in your teams:

1. **Get involved** – Be visibly present with the team. Do not lead a team that cannot see you.

2. **Stand in front** – Know that the buck stops with you, embrace the strengths and opportunities of the team and focus on what you will do to make them better.

3. **Be the example** – Do not expect more from others than you would from yourself. When things get

tough, teach the skills needed and be willing to do the work with the team.

4. **Understand the layers** – People process things differently. Embrace complexity. The right way does not have to be your way.

5. **Highlight your mistakes** – Do not hide your mistakes or your team will do the same. Use your mistakes to drive psychological safety and team growth.

Always commit to exploring different ways to sustain psychological safety within your team. The more your team sees your growth in how you recover from your mistakes, the more they will trust that

Poor performers will want to abuse your trust. Address them accordingly, but don't let one apple spoil the bunch. Hiding your mistakes to avoid shame will negatively impact team morale.

their mistakes are not something they need to hide. Be sure that your mistakes and the mistakes of others are used as learning opportunities.

Trust over Control

We are all guilty of believing that the way to do things must fit our thinking *exactly*. It is the "exactly part" that gets us in trouble as leaders. The desire to control everything will contradict your actions to build trust. Controlling someone's actions so they do things exactly as you would, with no freedom to change or evolve, will only result in outdated approaches and disengaged people. Have you ever wondered what it is like for everyone to agree with every decision you make? This can sound nice, until you realize that for some reason your team's performance results are never sustainable when conditions change. Consistently attempting to achieve goals by controlling the individual actions and thoughts of your team is not only counterproductive, but it also creates an illusion of a healthy and high-morale environment. If you have a team of people who all look and act exactly like you, please take a moment to check your ego at the door and make changes ASAP. Why – because chances are you and your team are already behind! Every organization faces shifts in customer demands, industry trends, and even employee needs. Control with no challenges from those you lead creates a false sense of security. Teamwork is about seeing problems from multiple angles and appreciating that there is more than one way to achieve an outcome and more opportunities to be mindful of on the horizon.

To make another sports analogy (I know, I love them all, well maybe just most of them), the coach of a sports team is vital to ensuring the team has direction. However, if that coach does not trust the insights and instincts of the players on the field, the team's ability

A coach has the power to control where the team goes. It is often difficult for a coach to predict every condition standing in the way of a win. Trust your team in those times; you might be impressed with what happens. Own the game, not the players, Coach!

to win diminishes. Successful coaches drive wins only when they trust their players, staff and resources. Their wins come when taking ownership to understand the game, not by limiting the players.

Empowerment versus Delegation

Coming off the coaching analogy sets us up to talk through the contrast between empowerment and delegation. While delegation is not inherently bad, there is more emphasis to drive control over trust. The wrong intent or delivery in your message when delegating work can indicate a lack of trust in a person to solve the problem in their own way. Now, when things go well, the checks and balances that need to come maintaining that morale do not matter as much. What about those situations that are not as clear cut, and the stakes are high? When a person is consistently awaiting your every direction to pass their thoughts and concerns to you, everyone loses sight of the goal, and everything is task driven with no end in sight. How can you pivot or adjust with any fluidity – you can't.

When you decide to empower someone, it is a remarkable success story for everyone. You get to collaborate throughout the journey and celebrate the win together with your team. Like we discussed in the engagement chapter, empowerment matters most when risks are high and the path to reaching the solution is not as clear. Empowerment is a result of establishing trust. Your ability to empower, especially in times of failure, exemplifies the value of trust and makes team success even more rewarding when it happens.

Empowerment Symptoms:

1. **Poise** – Positivity over panic. With active listening, patience, and well-timed urgency, show your team how a setback will not keep anyone down.

2. **Direct feedback** – Do not be afraid to call out what went wrong, but respond with context and substance, not bias.

3. **Forward thinking** – Focus on the next play. Show what needs to happen to get things back on track and what lessons everyone should learn.

These steps will demonstrate how much you trust their abilities without compromising accountability or lofty standards. Empowerment is a long game that tests your commitment to engage, build relationships, solve problems, and build team chemistry. It is also one of the best ways to learn about your successors. Come on, you didn't think you would be in the same leadership role forever, right?

As we close out this discussion on empowerment versus delegation, let me reiterate that step-by-step instructions are not entirely bad when using them as starting point or a guidepost and not a barrier. What I am cautioning you against are the "do it this way or else" leadership approaches. Empowerment uses teaching, mentorship, and humility as cornerstone philosophies to ensure you maintain a trust over control mindset.

...*there is no ceiling.*

If trust and empowerment are so important, why are they not visible in every work environment? It is a fair question to ask, but it is just as fair to appreciate this reality – *establishing and maintaining trust is work*! As we have discussed already, we all have egos and consistently putting our egos aside for others takes effort. Does a team with trust and empowerment have a ceiling? Some believe there is and the effort to establish trust is not worthwhile, especially if you can reach your goals without it. So, will trust and empowerment give a return on your investment? Hold that thought...

Picture this.... Have you ever wished for the opportunity to publicly display your skills, whether on the job, a sports team, or playing an instrument in front of a crowd or just a small group of friends? You are excited and nervous because you know some will appreciate you while others may judge you harshly. After showing what you can do, it is an even better feeling when you see others embrace your idea, cheer because you scored that point, or applaud because you played that note perfectly. The feeling you get from making an impact in the way you dreamt of it is beyond compare. Sometimes those accomplishments come with additional recognition, sometimes they do not, but either way, you seized an opportunity and influenced others. Now, your confidence is at an all-time high and with that confidence, the possibilities are endless. You cannot wait to build on what you did to make it even better next time. This is what it feels like when purpose and possibility come together. I hope you experience this feeling at some point in your life. Now imagine how a team of people with this same experience can do when striving to reach new heights. Why is this so important? What does this have to do with trust and empowerment? We started this conversation by asking if trust and empowerment have a ceiling. The answer is yes, but only if you allow it. How can you put a limit on trust and empowerment? By offering the chance for purpose and possibility to come together for only a few, and not for the many. Think about the eruption of confidence and the possibilities that come when feeling empowered. The benefits of that kind of support are beyond numerical calculations. The question of empowerment is not based on whether you *make* the investment, but more so asking how you do not *waste* the investment. Consider that thought as we move into the next part of our conversation (I'm so glad we have gotten this far). Connecting our trust and empowerment question to this next topic often comes with preconceived notions because of the excuses we all make to avoid uncomfortable dialogue. Let's push through that tension to address one of the most controversial yet necessary topics to ensure trust doesn't have a ceiling—**intentional diversity**.

Intentional diversity and why it matters

The importance of building trust in a team requires you to ask yourself tough questions that are uncomfortable for many people. So, let's ask ourselves: What is intentional diversity and why does it matter?

When looking up the definition of diversity, you will see many explanations centered around the inclusion of races, genders, ethnicities, and religions. Diversity in people considers all traits that make one individual different from another in some ways and the same in others. You have probably seen organizations launch new programs to express the importance of diversity in the workplace. You have also probably seen others remove the same programs for the same reason. Diversity programs aim to create connections and empathy, emphasizing that every culture is relevant and that all people matter. But again, what exactly is *intentional diversity* and why does it matter?

Trust, empowerment, and the ceiling for both are connected. The fastest way to limit trust in a team or organization is to limit the opportunity for empowerment to a few. The "few" I am referring to is not just the number of individuals on the team, but the diverse cultures reflected within the team. Putting a ceiling on cultural diversity (i.e. diverse cultural representation on a team) limits a leader's capacity to trust, empower, and learn from diverse perspectives.

How does that happen? Why would a leader intentionally limit their knowledge? It is because of that nasty b-word that no one likes to say – Bias.

Here are just a few ways in which we allow bias to dictate our environment:

1. Believing that bias is a thing of the past.

2. Assuming that a lack of cultural representation, especially in leadership, is just the norm and should not be a big deal.

3. Refusing to confront your own bias because of how it makes you feel.

4. Believing that something that does not bother you should not bother others.

5. Believing that when you see cultural diversity in prominent positions, the role went to someone underqualified.

Bias exists in every human being, both consciously and unconsciously. As humans, we naturally flock to those with similar interests and backgrounds. This behavior is not inherently bad, it is normal, but it becomes problematic when we defend our biases to avoid discomfort or to learn. A biased mindset can create a toxic working environment if not checked with intentionality. It can strip away empowerment and the joy of opportunity for others without you even realizing it. The longer it goes unchecked and the more excuses you make, the more your team sees your behavior as an indication of who you are and how you lead. Worse still, those aspiring to be your successor may replicate your bias, believing it to be the standard for success. Now you are left with a team that looks alike and thinks alike. It is tough stay on the cutting edge of anything and "think outside the box" if everyone on your team is so used to living inside one.

Use Intentional diversity to combat your bias. As a leader, you have an obligation to:

1. Challenge yourself on who makes up your team and why.

2. Observe your team's collaborative effort to see if everyone has a voice when talking through an opportunity.

3. Look at the culture representations of your team. Do not be afraid to ask yourself why your leadership team has a different cultural makeup than the people who do the work.

4. Take action to improve your organization's cultural representation and hold your leaders and peers accountable for the same.

5. Understand that a lack of cultural representation will directly limit how well you innovate.

Diversity is more than acknowledging unfamiliar cultures; it is about including those differences in decision-making processes. Any

It's not enough to not be a racist; being an ambassador for diversity means actively challenging biases.

attempt to highlight cultures without integrating them into

the actions and decisions of an organization is merely a futile attempt to check a box.

Intentional diversity holds us accountable for our biases. It is a continuous commitment to growing trust, empowerment and leading a team towards endless possibilities. Diversity should be a given, not an add-on or an initiative. You will know when it is present and when it is not. The question is, what will you do when it is not there? Are you willing to engage and challenge traditions? What kind of leader do you want to be?

I leave you with this: The best organizations in the world consistently innovate at the highest level because every layer of their organization is diverse. Check the data for yourself... Need I say more?

The power of trust is the lifeblood of your leadership actions. It affects your desire to understand and will drive your ability to engage with genuine intentions. Let the action of building trust drive every leadership action we discuss. When you do this, our next and final leadership action topic we discuss will seem that much clearer for you. It is now time to talk about our last leadership action – **translate**.

Translate

Translate versus Communicate

"Communication! We need to communicate better! You need to get better with your communication skills!"

How often do you hear someone go to those lines when something goes wrong? I can honestly say that we use the word *communication* so much that now it just takes the form of an overly used cliché. Of course, connecting with people, namely the ones you lead, requires you to communicate, but have you noticed that no matter how hard you try, sometimes the message just does not seem to get through. Ever experience times when you believe your message gets misinterpreted or unheard, and the immediate response is "try to work on your communication," as if you hadn't tried already? Does that phrase ever get under your skin? Trust me, you are not alone. I'm willing to believe that you tried hard to communicate the right way the first time. Now in no way am I trying to diminish the importance of working on your communication skills to connect with people. What I am calling out is the question of whether we know what it means to improve your communication as a leader.

This is a definition of communication I found when searching online:

> *"Communication applies to the exchange of ideas and thoughts within two or more individuals. It can be done through writing, speech, gestures, symbols, or written communication. Communication is a continuous transmission of a message among two or more individuals—the sender and receiver."* (LinkedIn, Dec 11, 2021)

What a beautifully crafted definition - nice and thorough. After we strip away the formality, communication is a way to connect anything together using any delivery method at our disposal. Because it is not clear who's responsible for the connection between the message giver versus the message receiver, we find ourselves constantly cycling through different ways to communicate until something sticks. Doesn't this sound like a lovely carousel of fun? How often have you witnessed in the workplace or the classroom where a teacher or a manager focuses solely on ensuring their message is visible and it is on you to just get it? If that approach truly worked with all the technology and social media available to us, we should be a unified world with misinterpretations being a thing of the past. Sharing information, however we want would be so much fun, because the message is bound to get through, right? I mean with all the media resources at our fingertips, if we all commit to sharing information repeatedly, we should all just eventually understand each other, right? When you communicate, I'm certain the reason people are not retaining what you say is mainly due to you leaving out the pertinent information. If you just added that extra word, sentence, or just had a stronger vocabulary, everyone would get what you're trying to say... Am I laying the sarcasm on a little thick? – My apologies...

There is an action that allows for connections to consistently happen without staying in a rotating hamster wheel of noisy, non-impactful communication. This action is often described in a similar fashion to the word communicate, but there is a distinct difference in the essence of the word and the outcomes it creates. So, let's put the word "communicate" on ice and replace it with a word that does a better job of bringing together our three other leadership actions; that word is **translate**.

You may have heard the word translate often used when learning a different language. Language translation is one of the best examples that comes to mind when thinking through the best ways to explain the difference between translation and communication. Think about translating any two languages (English to Spanish, German to Japanese, French to Hindi – you name it), often there is not a one-to-one connection for every word used in each language. This means the effort to connect requires us to use not just words, but depth in the form of body language and whatever is at our disposal to provide the right context needed to connect. Our initial thoughts in the words we choose to use may make sense to us, but without the proper context to clarify our points of view, our message will get lost in the dialogue, thereby creating that hamster wheel effect. Translation requires a commitment to using the right words with the right context. Using our foreign language example, at times you will struggle a bit finding the right words to say to illustrate your point of view. However, the effort you make to give context to your message, by being open to feedback and explaining your point of view, will motivate your audience to go the extra mile and extend their understanding to help you translate. This is the power of translation and why it is embraced universally and done so naturally. The effort you put into translation is the same approach used to build trust. This is what makes it so effective when establishing connections within your team or an organization. In leadership translation pushes you to understand the other side of an idea, connecting you and the team to the message. Translation is what brings to life your intent to establish understanding, engagement, and trust. Without trust, translation cannot occur, and you are left with a failed communication cycle that never ceases. Communication is a commitment to contact; translation is a commitment to connect.

Planning, Storytelling, Strategy

Think back to a bad movie, lecture, book (hopefully not this one), webcast, meeting—you name it. How easy is it to tie your response to that experience with bad storytelling? You just couldn't follow the presenter's point and there was no connection you could make to the story being told. Now hold that thought and think through the dialogue you have with your team, better yet, the dialogue you observe within your team. When you see your team collectively working, do they resemble a group that has a clear understanding of what their work means to themselves, each other, or the industry? Do you see each of them supporting one another to achieve common goals you set out for them to achieve? If so, then you can safely assume your leadership message is translating throughout your team with effective storytelling. If you cannot answer these questions confidently and your team is not working together with cohesion, trust, and clear outcomes, then there is a good chance that your message has not translated into their work environment. So, what do you do when that happens? What are the telling signs when your engagement efforts don't seem to be enough? Remember the part of our engagement discussion where we talked about the importance of planning and strategy? This is where it matters. Your mission and strategy messages need to translate within your team. Your mission is the outcome, and the strategy is your plan. Both must exist in more ways than just posters on a wall or website. Your mission and strategy need to tell a story. Storytelling is another exercise to build trust in others (told you trust is always the glue) so they can connect to where you are trying to lead them. Storytelling allows you to build trust by connecting your team's purpose to the plans and the outcomes you believe must come to life. This is a responsibility in leadership that we all take for granted. Always look at your plans and ask yourself if they tell a cohesive story. What's a cohesive story? A story that allows your team to connect the goals you have with the ones they have for themselves. Leverage the work and camaraderie you have with your team as daily validation of that story. Every obstacle you overcome together will test their alignment to your plan and even help you assess how well your leadership lives within the pulse of your team. Sounds a little like engagement, doesn't it? Translation and storytelling go hand in hand to give you leadership actions a voice. The more effective you are in exercising your other leadership actions (Understand, engage, trust), the more impactful and easier your translations will be.

The Art of Translation

Translating a message to ensure your team stays connected is more about effort than vocabulary. Memorizing every word and definition in the dictionary won't provide insight into the right words to use for every person, every time. The art of translation is about building trust in your message and seeking to understand methods and connections that ensure your message consistently resonates with people. You may wonder about the kind of work that goes into building your translation capabilities. Check out these *Translation Principles* and see how well they work for you.

Translation Principles:

1. Keep everyone involved. Always know how your story/mission/vision translates to everyone on the team. Commit to understanding how and why the message you want to send will connect with others.

2. The work is constant. Continue to refine your translation methods by seeking feedback and learning the needs of your team.

3. Avoid looking at translation from a single lens. Do not be afraid to pivot from your point of view when you receive new information.

4. Make the team a part of the change. Give your team insight into why a change is necessary. Change is scary at times. This removes that fear!

5. Translation does not always require you to speak. Listen, and learn when not to talk. This is important as any method you can use to translate and build trust within your team.

Translation is as much an art as it is an action. You are not perfect, and your team knows that. Learning is growth. When you embrace growth with a positive response, especially growth that stems from failure, you instill confidence in others. This is a vital way to build connections with others and prevent the need to show yourself as the hero. Besides, comeback stories are the most influential when the team can share in the victory. When a member of your team observes you applying these principles for the sake of others, you will be surprised at the appreciation and trust that emerges in everyone. Put forth a genuine effort to apply these principles. You will find that these deposits will go a long way to establish the trust, empowerment, and engagement you need to be a trusted leader.

The Willingness and Ability to Teach.

Growing and developing team members is not the hardest idea for a leader to grasp. Honestly, who would publicly deny that developing others is what you should do as part of leadership? The bigger question to consider is how do you know when your teaching methods are growing someone's skills versus you just taking the easy way out to delegate a problem away? We talked earlier about the importance of providing opportunities to others. So, once we do that, we can check that box and declare ourselves leaders, right? Hey, you provided the opportunity. That is sufficient evidence to confidently say you are developing someone. With all due respect to many swim instructors, throwing someone who cannot swim into the deep end of the pool and walking away does not make you an instructor. It is also not a great way to develop a strong swimmer. The responsibility of leadership includes a genuine willingness to teach. Without that, you are just delegating problems away to save yourself some time.

So how do you know when you are developing and not just delegating?

Think through your leadership actions and answer for yourself:

Do you understand the skills you are trying to develop? How will the opportunity you present grow that team member according to their goals and achieve the outcomes you need? Never shy away from making an opportunity a win-win for you and the team member.

Do you engage consistently to ensure the people you lead are set up for success? Give people a chance to showcase their abilities. Embrace the complexities that come with collaborating with different learning styles. This will drive your mindset to better embrace innovative thinking, new technologies, and ever-changing market conditions.

Do you trust that with success will come failure? Let people learn from their failures without feeling the need to take over. Embrace success and failure as learning opportunities and springboards for the next challenge. One of your best rewards as a leader is seeing how your team responds to adversity.

Do you translate your messages to ensure the work connects with the people? Do not just deliver information, then micromanage along the way. Schedule check-ins to reinforce the progress of the plan and be open to receiving feedback from the teams responsible for the work.

Use these thought questions to develop your team with genuine intentions. This method of translation creates a cycle of empowerment that enables a team to overcome any challenge with a positive and collaborative mindset.

EMPOWERMENT CYCLE

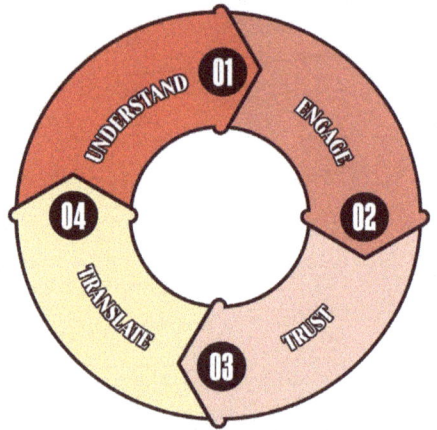

01 Ensure team outcomes connect to an individual's growth.

02 Set everyone up for sucess.

03 Remove the fear of failure.

04 Choose dialogue and feedback over micromanagement.

Always keep your translation skills at the forefront of your leadership actions so that your team stays connected. Translation is the voice you give your actions and what inspires others to do the same. Embrace it!

As we end

Laying it all on the line....

I am told that a fundamental rule in wrapping up a conversation is to summarize the conversation and not to introduce any new viewpoints...Well maybe this will not come off as a new idea, but more of a point of emphasis before we leave. We have talked about the actions of leadership that can lead to career success, which I define as achieving business outcomes and, more importantly, building and sustaining trust and morale. Committing to both in the ways that we've discussed is not easy, no matter how much you talk about the desire to do them. Leadership is both hard and rewarding. There will be good days, bad days, awesome days, and days that will just seem overwhelming. In all that we have discussed, I hope that there is a lot you can take away, but if you had to choose just one lesson, let it be this:

Being a great leader will require you to lay it all on the line...

Every leader faces tough decisions, decisions where you will stand alone and make a call that may not be the most popular or the easiest to predict the outcome. At times, these decisions will be uncomfortable, nerve-wracking, and risky. If these are not feelings you have had as a leader yet, then this is the perfect time to ask yourself if you are being pushed or pushing yourself enough. We have said numerous times now, taking a team to the next level of anything worthwhile starts and ends with you. The work you put into understanding, engagement, trust, and translation will give you the confidence and credibility you need for others to follow your lead and support you when failure occurs. Building these actions in yourself and your team instills confidence in everyone when facing the unknown and when making risky decisions. When applying these actions, your team will walk through the fire with you because they know you will do the same for them every day. Bring your complete self to work, regardless of the risk. Stay humble and stay learning as you have done throughout this discussion, but more importantly, never stop being yourself. Establishing this standard is the best testament of confidence that your team will see in you and as a result, they and others will do the same. All that we have discussed today will prepare you for these moments, where risk, fear, and failure are overcome by confidence, trust, and strong leadership. Decades of experience have shown me this dynamic to be true time and time again. Accept this challenge. Do not ever be afraid to lay it all on the line… You owe that much to your team and yourself.…

Until next time…

I hope that my growth over the past fifteen years has made this conversation much more rewarding than our first. As you go through your leadership journey, I hope this discussion has answered enough questions for you to continue blazing your own trail as a leader. More importantly, I hope this discussion has prompted new questions for you to ask yourself—questions you had not originally considered in your leadership journey. If so, then I accomplished my goal. New ideas and questions should arise from the answers you find. That is the beauty of collaboration, creativity, innovation, and of course, leadership. As you continue to walk into your leadership journey, think about what you need to better **understand** your leadership purpose and what you need to always **engage** with your team. **Trust** that your mistakes will lead to future success and always commit to **translate** for others. Finally, know that **diversity is a given** and when that is a core part of your leadership recipe, you will never need to add it later. Diversity is the cake, not the icing.

Continue to take on challenges that others might think are over your head. How else will you reach new heights if you don't?

I hope you've gained more clarity on what it means to be an impactful leader—by action, not by title.

I really appreciate the time, friend. I hope you can say the same...

References

https://www.linkedin.com/pulse/what-best-definition-communication-milad-azami/

About the Author

Alcott Alda Hekima Germany II, a proud Detroit native, brings over two decades of leadership experience across diverse industries, including automotive, consumer products, telecommunications, and financial services. Having worked with renowned companies such as Procter & Gamble, BASF, and Rocket Companies, Alcott is widely recognized for his ability to cultivate leaders, build dynamic teams, and craft strategies that drive real results.

Alcott holds a bachelor's degree in chemical engineering from the University of Detroit Mercy and a master's degree in education from the University of Phoenix. His unique blend of technical expertise and passion for teaching fuels his deep commitment to personal and professional development.

As the author of *Real World 101: Student Guide*—now available in more than 10 languages—Alcott has inspired a global audience. The book is celebrated as a practical, empowering resource that equips readers of all ages with the tools needed to succeed in real-life situations.

In addition to his writing, Alcott is a dynamic public speaker known for motivating audiences through powerful stories and actionable insights. His engaging presence and ability to foster meaningful connections empower individuals to envision their goals and take concrete steps toward achieving them.

Whether through his books or his speaking engagements, Alcott Germany II is dedicated to helping others unlock their full potential and thrive in every aspect of life.

Learn more about Alcott Germany II at www.alcottgermanyii.com